# The Hunters of Domesticated Love

## Tales of Violence (+18)

### Hugo Jepsen

# Chapters

# Warning (+18)

Abuse, violence and other similar subjects are described in this book.

# Preface

The story of 'The Hunters of Domesticated Love' revolves around the
main character — let's call him Peter, or let's call her Grace since the
gender is omitted in the book's content.

Peter or Grace — begin a relationship with a man who has narcissistic
and bad-tempered behaviours. From burning desire to absolute
extremes of violence; this story written in poetry speaks of their feelings,
emotions, and selected events of the relationship and how it all ends.

This story is not based on my personal experience or inspired by —
simply by pure imagination.

*Enjoy and read with care!*

# painfully alive

I've never been alive,
always lived in my head.
Safer to see through my lenses,
drunk or high or the same as dead.

I am back to see my friends —
let's hit the dirty streets
while the full moon shines over it
because the night belongs to me.

Born to want to feel pleasure
but I've been staying for the pain,
I don't carry much work experience
but rumours were attributed to my name.

Mother said I work against God's will,
but that's now how He makes me feel.
And I hate to admit that I'm right
because I'm never sure of something in life.

# selfish I am

Say to me you love me,
selfish I am all the time
but deep within,
I know I cross your mind.

And if you decide to come,
I'm sure that I will run
because I can't understand
how to be loved by a man.

The scent of your cologne
is stinking in my clothes
and your pain has become
a token to my oath.

When I was young,
I was pretty and free,
but things have changed
and I'm no longer who I used to be.

# pale skin

Cold hands of mine,
eerie sounds I make -
what's in my mind?

Going ablaze for it all
for reasons unknown
since freezing waters
is what I've always drunk.

A path that leads me astray,
stubborn in my behaviour,
wanting things my way.

Pretty in your eyes,
attractive to your body,
barely do you know I hate what's mine.

# unknown tenderness

A monster in your bed
is what I think I am -
a hunter of hearts
coming for me again.

Little stars twinkling
at the back of your wall
is my telepathy
trying to give you a call.

Please, wake up,
we need to talk
about this love.

Don't make me wait
because while I do so,
my blood grows cold
my emotions get easily sold.

# pontific

What I hate to admit
is that somebody out there
might want to be in love with me.

That's because I can't feel
anything at all, nothing at all.
I am afraid to break someone's heart
because I know how much it hurts
to be abandoned while still in love.

I've been waiting for you
but I need to tell you I'm not ready
for the wild things, you want me to do.

I'm not an angel, I'm not a saint,
so don't pray for me to come close -
I've got blood attached to my name,
the only thing I truly love is pain.

Walking on these streets
looking alive when I'm dead.
You've sanctified me instead
of seeing me for who I am.

# domesticated like an animal

I used to tell you the future
but you've cut my tongue -
put me to clean your room
to think about what I had done.

When you came home
everything was ready for your sleep.
My body bleeding out of tiredness
because you sexualized me.

I cannot see you when you
tie my arms around my back
because you need me to
forget the mistakes of your past.

Everything that I once knew
has changed completely.
And I know your point of view -
it was easier to domesticate the beast
that lives inside the spectrum I see through.

# cruel bed

Bring your green cigarettes -
happiness is something that I
need as a tool to pretend
that fun is what I'm having in bed.

Tied me down so I couldn't move,
and told me that I was careless when
I gave up on life to be in love with you.

Something is craving more
and the sun finally has come,
I thought my despair was finished
but as long as I'm not dead, you're not done.

Praying to the gods with tears on my face
while I feel your push and your pull -
there's some beauty in achieving
the patience to deal with the cruel.

# light in squares

Since I've left you in that house,
I thought that running enough
but others threw me into a tower
and told me, I cursed you, my love.

What is it now? I thought freedom
was something completely different
from what I am experiencing now -
the flowers have lost their colour
and I'm unsure of what I know about.

Come here and tell me that I'm wrong,
I've done the worst thinking what
I was doing was for the best
and life cycled me back to setbacks -
I am dreadfully haunted by the past.

# dishonest melancholy

I've perished a thousand times
thinking that all I had in mind
was an exuberant story of blame
when all I've ever done was sane.

Every page that I've ever written
was inspired by the muse
but the truth of it all
is that I wrote inspirations based upon you.

I run the forests while stuck on its vines,
one housing row in front of me for me to live
thinking that freedom was the Eden of life.

They put a wooden box upon my head,
whipped the very veins of my body,
random spits telling me I wasn't a real human
and all of this for the sake of dishonest melancholy.

# **blackening** out here

Neck with purple stains on it,
throat threw into a cold stone,
far away from the despairs of home.

I hear people shouting
while my eyes are closed -
if I could, I would leave this place,
but they've tied me down strongly enough.

A few more seconds into meeting the afterlife,
I've waited for so long - for so long for this -
my thought process when I used to be
wrapped in the nest of your bedsheets.

I don't hear the cut but I felt the axe,
I think that I don't exist anymore -
it's blackening out here, my love.
Where do we go after leaving this Earth?

# godly gifts

A singing that sounds so eerie,
I can almost hear it with my ears
if at least, I was left with any.

My body moves so fast
but I didn't even make a move -
my heart isn't burning through you.

It's a place where I'm arriving at,
a movie scene of all of my past -
brutally honest, brutally pretty,
God gifted me with such wild beauty.

# heavenly endings -8-

Hornets crying sounds for me,
deep within the dark lights of life,
got caught out in a rainstorm -
would you hear me if I try to cry?

It's all gone wrong but when
despair is what I felt,
heaven has lent me its hand.

The broken skies can unleash
forces I've never seen before
and what was once peace
is now endless endorse.

Give me a sign and tell me
if love was ever its worth
of fighting for because I'm not sure.

The stakes of my life were high,
I told myself too many lies
to give meaning to my life.

The image of me has disappeared.
The image of me doesn't exist anymore.
I met the end... I met... hold on! Who am I?

# Bonus Chapters

# my anxiety is destroying our relationship

I carved in a tree, your name,
so my heart can find a stable ground
when your passion makes me feel insane.

You've given up the heaven above,
so you could save me from the hell I live in -
if that is not love, what then? what is it?

I just want to live in this moment forever,
but I'm afraid if I don't get any better,
I'll be missing out on us being together.

And I apologize for all the mistakes,
my anxiety is destroying our relationship -
and I am so sorry.

# assumptions of love

Soaking up in tears,
if I'm mistaken, I apologize
but there's something in your eyes
that got my heart hypnotized.

All these assumptions made -
going too fast, going too slow -
and if I cared just a little,
that's not what I feel in my soul.

And alone - glistening in the rain -
all these flowers growing up on the roof.
If I could climb the ladder to get them,
I'd pick them up to decorate your room.

If that's not enough - What is then?
If that's not love - How do you know?
What do people say? - Are they happy again?
I don't think so, I do not think so.

# I just know how I feel

The smell of the fish in the sea -
somewhat agonizing but refreshing -
that's the lenses which you see through me.

Antagonizing - summer strikes -
one blow of wind at a time,
and every time it gets violent,
it violates my state of mind.

If I could change, I would,
it's not in my nature
to not be at peace -
I rather just leave.

It's penetrating my soul,
knots filled with thorns,
pain is all I've ever known.

You ask me for love in return,
I'd give you so if I could
but I don't know how to -
I just know that I'm in love with you.

# abyss

I went to the abyss the other day
to try to find something rare -
what I only found was
my own spectrum of despair.

Negligence is the word I miss out
every time someone gets close to me,
but if despair wasn't what I had found,
perhaps, I'd have someone on my knees.

Careless was the apathy that consumed
all the potential gains, I could've won,
but instead, I made the mistake
of trying to solve realism alone.

I came back to the abyss once again,
I think I'll stay here for quite a while,
hoping that someone would have the courage
to meet me, even when I feel hostile.

# you've been changing but it's not enough

You said you can do it all night,

said that I was walking out of line,

but I can't make any excuses for you,

and for you, I can't put my trauma to the side.


Had me feeling like I've died,

I've never seen a man cry

like when I saw myself do, so,

and the fault is yours - you know?


And I see, you've been changing,

trying to be more of my taste.

And I see, you've been chasing,

but I think now it's far too late.


And you know, you messed me up,

we'll never be friends like this,

hating me, won't make me love,

wanting me, it's nothing special,

exes like you and me don't become sexual.

# it's ending, it's fine

As if I could touch the sky
with both of my eyes -
as if I could just breathe
inside of me with peace.

But it's now how it goes,
flavours of insecurities
is all I've ever known.

And you've seen the best,
and you've seen the worst -
are you sure you love me?
Are you? Are you sure?

It's ending, it's fine,
it's not like I'm not sad
but I learned that it's life -
the X point in time.

# Credits

Writer: Hugo Jepsen
Editor: Hugo Jepsen
Cover Creator: Hugo Jepsen
Image License: Unsplash
Publisher: Amazon

# Disclaimer

Any resemblance to other creative projects is mere coincidence.

# Copyrights

Protected and Licensed with a Copyright Infringement.